The Hip-hop Scene

The Stars ♪ The Fans ♪ The Music

Ann Graham Gaines and Reggie Majors

Enslow Publishers, Inc.
40 Industrial Road
Box 398
Berkeley Heights, NJ 07922
USA

http://www.enslow.com

Library of Congress Cataloging-in-Publication Data
Gaines, Ann.
  The hip-hop scene : the stars, the fans, the music / Ann Graham Gaines and Reggie Majors.
     p. cm. — (The music scene)
  Includes bibliographical references and index.
  Summary: "Read about the music, stars, clothes, contracts, and world of hip-hop music"—Provided by publisher.
  ISBN-13: 978-0-7660-3396-2
  ISBN-10: 0-7660-3396-1
  1. Rap (Music)—History and criticism—Juvenile literature. I. Majors, Reggie. II. Title.
  ML3531.G35 2009
  782.421649—dc22

                          2008048010

Printed in the United States of America

10 9 8 7 6 5 4 3 2 1

To Our Readers:
This text has not been authorized by the musicians or bands mentioned throughout this book.

       We have done our best to make sure all Internet addresses in this book were active and appropriate when we went to press. However, the author and the publisher have no control over and assume no liability for the material available on those Internet sites or on other Web sites they may link to. Any comments or suggestions can be sent by e-mail to comments@enslow.com or to the address on the back cover.

♻ Enslow Publishers, Inc., is committed to printing our books on recycled paper. The paper in every book contains 10% to 30% post-consumer waste (PCW). The cover board on the outside of each book contains 100% PCW. Our goal is to do our part to help young people and the environment too!

Cover Photo Credit: WireImage/Getty Images
Interior Photo Credits: Alamy/Nancy Ney/Digital Vision, p. 17; Alamy/Content Mine International, p. 20; AP Photo/Jeff Christensen, p. 7; Chris Berkey, p. 33; Corbis/Laura Levine, p. 25; Corbis/Steve Azzara, p. 30; Getty Images/Theo Wargo/ WireImage, p. 12; Getty Images/Kevin Winter, p. 19; Getty Images/Jemal Countess/WireImage, pp. 22, 23; Getty Images/Frank Micelotta, p. 36; The Image Works/Margot Granitsas, p. 8; The Image Works/Topham, p. 21; The Image Works/Jeff Greenberg, p. 38; The Image Works/Gloria Wright/ Syracuse Newspapers, p. 39; The Image Works/Syracuse Newspapers/G Walts, p. 41; iStockphoto.com/Alexander Hafemann, p. 10; Landov/Lucas Jackson/Reuters, pp. 1, 14, 15; Landov/Isaac Brekken/UPI, p. 9; Landov/Mario Anzuoni/Reuters, pp. 31, 34; Landov/Robert Galbraith/Reuters, p. 40; Retna Ltd./ John Ricard, p. 2; Retna Ltd./Gene Ambo, p. 4; Retna Ltd./Jackie Butler, p. 5; Retna Ltd./Joe Conzo, p. 6; Retna Ltd./Tara Canova, p. 18; Retna Ltd./Michael Benbib, p. 27; Retna Ltd./John Ricard, p. 28.

Cover: *Kanye West performs at Madison Square Garden in New York City in 2008.*

Right: *Soulja Boy does his signature dance at a BET New Year's Eve party.*

Contents

❶ *Hot Stuff*

Hip-hop. Thirty years ago, this wasn't even a word. Today we use *hip-hop* to describe an extremely popular kind of music—and a way of life. Hip-hop is so widely known that a *National Geographic* article recently said we're living on a "hip-hop planet."[1]

What's HOT

What's hot in hip-hop? In the United States, *Lil Wayne* and *Kanye West* rule the hip-hop scene. In 2009, Lil Wayne won four Grammy Awards. Lots of Americans also love old favorites *Missy Elliott*, *Snoop Dogg*, and *Gnarls Barkley*.

Lil Wayne is one of today's hip-hop megastars.

Americans also follow hip-hop stars who are from outside the United States. One example is **M.I.A.** She grew up in Sri Lanka, a country next to India.

Always *Changing*

Fans stay interested in hip-hop because it constantly reinvents itself. Artists blend hip-hop with other kinds of music. **Daddy Yankee** introduced Americans to a new sound from the Caribbean. His hit song "Gasolina" is an example of reggaeton. This type of music mixes hip-hop with Caribbean rhythms.

M.I.A. is a popular hip-hop artist from Sri Lanka.

Rap *v.* Hip-hop

What's the difference between rap and hip-hop? People get confused because the two types of music overlap. Rap is a type of music with words spoken over a strong beat. Musician **Rob Swift** says rap is a type of hip-hop. But he believes hip-hop is way more than just music: "When you say hip-hop, you say graffiti, you say break dancing, you say DJs, MCs, the way you dress, the way you talk—all the elements, all in one."[2]

2 *Ultimate Style*

Hip-hop has a look of its own. Young people from all over the world dress like hip-hop stars. At high schools in Iowa and parks in Tokyo, you can see boys wearing baggy pants, big sports jerseys, and expensive sneakers.[3]

HOT *Threads*

Hip-hop has always had its own fashion. It started with break-dancers, who traveled with an MC's show. They wore oversize cargo shorts and slick bomber jackets as they spun on the floor or on a piece of cardboard. Sneakers provided traction. To add a layer of cool, dancers wore Kangol bucket hats and, later, wave caps.

When MCs wanted to spread a message, they added a new element of style. *Afrika Bambaataa* showed pride in his heritage by wearing a dashiki and dreadlocks. In her video for "Ladies First," *Queen Latifah* wore red, green, and black clothing. These colors are often worn in Africa.

Afrika Bambaataa's clothing shows pride in his heritage.

Got to Have
BLING

When hip-hop artists began to earn big money, their style changed. They started to show off by wearing bling—large, glitzy jewelry and mouth grills. Two clothing styles emerged. Clean-cut stars *DJ Jazzy Jeff & The Fresh Prince* chose designer clothes in bright colors. Other artists started to dress like they were in prison. They wore baggy pants because prison inmates aren't allowed to have belts.

In the 1990s, designer Tommy Hilfiger got rich selling to the hip-hop crowd. Some artists even started their own clothing lines. *Diddy* (Sean Combs) owns the Sean John label. Phat Farm belongs to *Russell Simmons*. *Nelly*, *50 Cent*, *Snoop Dogg*, and *M.I.A.* also have their own clothing brands.

Air Force Ones

Shoes are a big part of hip-hop gear. Break-dancers of the 1970s wore Chuck Taylors. In the 1980s, hip-hop fans started to wear Nikes, Adidas, and Reeboks. When Nelly had a megahit with his song "Air Force Ones," these Nike shoes became more popular than ever. Hip-hop fans also like to wear boots, especially Timberlands.

(Left to right:) Famous, Slick Rick, and Chamillionaire sport some bling.

A New Kind of Art

Hip-hop style is more than just clothing and jewelry. For example, the culture inspired a completely new art form called graffiti, also called tagging. Hip-hop music was born in New York City, where taggers marked their territory by spray painting symbols on walls. In the 1970s, more artistic graffiti began to replace these tags. It appeared everywhere— on buildings, fences, highway overpasses, and subway cars.

Some people dislike graffiti. Others see it as an art. By the mid-1980s, graffiti artists were showing their work in art galleries. Today, some graffiti artists get paid to decorate buildings—a major turnaround!

The owner of this building complex in Queens, New York, welcomes graffiti artists to share their artwork.

> *Cars are a big part of hip-hop style. Here, 50 Cent shows off his customized Pontiac G8.*

Cool **Rides**

Hip-hop artists often rap about cars. In the 1970s, ***DJ Kool Herc*** put oversize speakers in the back seat of his convertible and drove around neighborhoods playing his music to advertise his next show. Today some artists buy big cars like Hummers, with expensive sound systems and DVD players. Other hip-hop stars buy classic cars and fit them out with rims, spinners, and fancy paint jobs.

Hip-hop Dictionary
Hip-hop has its own vocabulary. Words and phrases that MCs use make it into everyday talk. Fans use language like **chillax** *(a blend of* **chill** *and* **relax***),* **the hood, bling,** *and giving and getting* **props** *(respect).*

9

Break dancing is one of hip-hop's major contributions to the entertainment world.

③ Dance!

In the early days of hip-hop, the biggest stars were the dancers. Up on stage, a DJ played music for people to dance to. The DJ picked out breaks—the hottest, most rhythmic parts of a song—that made people want to move. Sometimes an MC rapped over the music to get the crowd even more involved.

But people's attention was focused down front—on the b-boys (short for *break boys*) and the b-girls. Break dancing was born on the street in the late 1970s. Dancers blend fancy footwork with acrobatic moves. They spin on their knees and even their heads.

B-boys formed crews. The most important early dance crew was the **Rock Steady Crew**, which got started in 1977.

On the Dance Floor

In the 1970s, hip-hop adopted two other styles of dance— poppin' and lockin'. These moves changed into dances like the robot and the cabbage patch.

Today, dance crazes pop up and fade away. Fans learn the latest moves on television and online. In 2007, the Superman dance performed to "Crank That (Soulja Boy)" by **Soulja Boy** took off after a video got posted on YouTube.

Getting Crunk
When you're "crunk," you're all cranked up—and you just gotta dance. Some of today's biggest hip-hop names are from the South, and they have their own brand of music. It's made to be danced to—very fast, with a big bass beat. When dancers get crunk, they shake like crazy.

Mary J. Blige lights up the stage at Madison Square Garden on her 2008 tour with Jay-Z.

4 On the Road

Mary J. Blige is called the Queen of Hip-hop Soul. Blige has had a lot of experience on the road. She often tours right after she releases a new album. When she and *Jay-Z* headed out on their Heart of the City Tour in March 2008, Blige's album *Growing Pains* was still at the top of the charts.

The Call of the Road

Blige starts to get ready for a tour even before her new album is on store shelves.

Months before, she meets with designers and choreographers. Together they decide on lighting, videos, and dance steps. Blige wants her shows to look great.

On tour, Blige works day after day. Her 2003 *Love & Life* tour took her all over the United States, to Sweden, and to Japan. The pace was relentless. Blige performed every other day. Six tour buses carried her staff, equipment, and luggage. At each destination, she gave a round of interviews with radio stations, newspaper reporters, and fans.

Under the Lights

On performance night, Blige had to get to the stadium or concert hall a couple of hours early to warm up and get her hair and makeup done. Every concert was two hours long. She changed her costume three times, with the help of people known as quick-change artists. Looking back, Blige remembers how tired she sometimes felt. But she also remembers how rewarded she felt.[4]

Blige especially loves pleasing her female fans. She says, "I love the fact that I'm doing something that makes an ocean of women get up on their feet."[5]

Fans show their love for Kanye West at a live show in California.

5 Live!

There is nothing like the excitement of going to a live hip-hop concert. What should you expect?

The biggest shows are held in huge arenas or sports stadiums. At most big shows, you'll see just a few people on stage. You'll see the MC and one or more DJs running the record players and mixers. There might be some backup singers, dancers, or other musicians. On his Glow in the Dark tour, **Kanye West** had a band that played below him in an orchestra pit.[6]

The Booming Bass

Expect the music to be very loud. You will feel the booming bass beats. At the same time, you

14

will see exciting light shows. Lights flash and change colors. Sometimes videos appear on a huge screen.

Audiences really get into it! Fans leave their seats and crowd together by the stage. There they follow the lead of the MCs, who lead a call and response. Many hip-hop fans shout and sing along as the stars perform.

Small Stage, Big Energy

The biggest shows can be expensive. Tickets sell for between $50 and $100. If you don't have that kind of money, don't worry. There are lots of ways to see hip-hop live. There are shows for adults at clubs and bars. Today you can also find family-friendly hip-hop shows sponsored by libraries, schools, city parks, camps, churches, and many other organizations.

One fun annual event is the Brooklyn Hip-Hop Festival, an entire month of hip-hop events in the summer. You can see hip-hop movies or go to poetry slams. On the last day, there are free concerts at a park under the Brooklyn Bridge. It's a great place to go with your family.[7]

6 *Ear Candy*

All day, every day. That's when hip-hop fans want to listen to their music!

On the Air

Millions of hip-hop fans listen to the radio. Today there are hip-hop stations in big American cities like New York and Los Angeles. Lots of other radio stations put hip-hop shows in their schedules. Internet and satellite radio stations also play lots of hip-hop. People can listen to shows broadcast from all over the world.

Digital Hip-hop

Many fans listen to hip-hop music on MP3 players. People still buy hip-hop CDs, but they also buy and download individual songs online. How do fans decide what music to buy? Lots of times, it's word of mouth. In person or on blogs, fans trade tips about the latest and greatest.

Keeping It *Safe*

Maybe you want to buy hip-hop music, but your parents object. They've heard that hip-hop music contains swear words and talks about inappropriate subjects. That can be true sometimes, but it's *not* true of all hip-hop. Plenty of the music is all right for kids to listen to. You can buy cleaned-up versions of hip-hop music at large chain stores or on the Web.

IMPORTANT TIP:

Never ask friends to copy songs for you. Don't make copies for other people, either. This is illegal. It's also illegal to download songs from file-sharing Web sites. Artists deserve to be paid for their music. When you download songs illegally, you are stealing their work. If you get caught, you and your parents could face heavy fines.

Hip-hop star Run-DMC and the rock band Aerosmith worked together to make their hit remix "Walk This Way."

7 *Hottest Videos*

When the video channel MTV started in 1981, it did not even show hip-hop videos. But after Black Entertainment Television (BET) attracted lots of viewers, MTV executives changed their minds. In 1988, a new show called *Yo! MTV Raps* went on the air. Soon MTV started a channel just for hip-hop fans.

Rock This Way

Another hip-hop video became famous when **Run-DMC** and **Aerosmith** remixed Aerosmith's song "Walk This Way." This funny video starts with Aerosmith on stage at an awards ceremony. Run-DMC listens from the other side of a wall.

Run-DMC starts to make too much noise. One of the rockers gets so mad that he uses his microphone stand to break the wall down. In the end, Run-DMC joins Aerosmith on stage, and the performers show that rock and hip-hop can live together.

Just Rewards

MTV gave its first rap video award to **DJ Jazzy Jeff & The Fresh Prince** for "Parents Just Don't Understand" in 1989. Today MTV has a hip-hop video award, too. The first one was given to the **Beastie Boys** for "Sabotage" in 1999. In 2007, **Rihanna** won the MTV Video of the Year Award for "Umbrella."[8]

How do today's fans find hip-hop videos? They tune in to MTV, VH1, and BET. Some artists release DVDs as well as CDs—for example, **Jay-Z**'s *Fade to Black*. In the last couple of years, the Internet has been the place to go for videos.

Rihanna accepts an MTV Video Music Award in 2007.

8 *On the Big Screen*

Go to the movies a few times, and you're probably going to hear hip-hop. Recent movies like *Freedom Writers* (2007), *Barbershop* (2002), *Honey* (2003), and *Stomp the Yard* (2007) have lots of hip-hop songs on their soundtracks. Even kids' movies get in on the action—think of the little penguin rapping in *Happy Feet* (2006).

Hip-hop Up Front

Sometimes you get to *see* hip-hop culture on the big screen, too. *Boyz N the Hood* (1991),

Boyz N the Hood *is a popular movie about hip-hop culture. Shown here are Ice Cube (left) and Cuba Gooding, Jr. (right).*

Save the Last Dance (2001), and *Hustle and Flow* (2005) are all movies about hip-hop artists. Sometimes real hip-hop stars, like **Snoop Dogg**, do the acting.

Documentaries are special kinds of movies. Rather than telling made-up stories, they are about real life. There have been many documentaries made about hip-hop. One of the most popular of all time is *Wild Style*, which was made in the Bronx in 1983. Some documentaries are biographies. There are several about **Tupac Shakur**, a rapper who was killed in a drive-by shooting in 1996.

9 First Moments

According to many sources, hip-hop was invented by a Jamaican immigrant named **DJ Kool Herc** in the summer of 1973. He started out using his father's PA system.

Herc first played a block party to help his sister, **Pep 1**, raise money.[9] He landed some indoor jobs and began making money. He also did free outdoor shows to give back to his neighborhood. He added reggae, funk, and disco to his blues, pop, and rock beats. Most important was his invention of break beats.

Hip-hop pioneer DJ Kool Herc

Afrika Bambaataa

Another important early DJ was **Afrika Bambaataa**. Inspired by Kool Herc, Bambaataa decided to host his own hip-hop parties. His sound included Afro-Caribbean rhythms and American rock. A former gang member,

Bambaataa formed the Zulu Nation, an organization that helps young people escape gang life.

Other Early DJs

Other important people in hip-hop history are **DJ Grand Wizard Theodore**, the first artist to "scratch," and **Coke La Rock**, one of the first MCs. La Rock's catchy sayings, such as "Raise your hands in the air, and wave 'em like you just don't care," became standard in the hip-hop world.

DJ Grand Wizard Theodore remembers the day he invented scratching. He was playing loud music. "My mom came bangin' on the door to turn it down," he said.[10] Instead, he put his hand on his record to stop the sound and then moved the record back and forth. He liked the sound so much that he introduced the "scratch" at a party. It was an instant hit.

Spreading Like Wildfire

The first recordings by early hip-hop artists were cassette tapes, which they gave to friends or sold on the street. Then record companies started to look for artists willing to make a record. But most artists were just focused on playing live.[11]

Put a Label on It

Then everything changed. It was 1979. A woman named **Sylvia Robinson** started a record label and signed the **Sugar Hill Gang**, who put out "Rapper's Delight." The song became a huge international hit and showed that hip-hop could make money. Other record companies began to look for hip-hop acts.

Another milestone occurred in 1981, when **Grandmaster Flash and the Furious Five** released "The Message." This song talks about the terrible conditions of urban slum life. This was the first LP record with live scratching and DJing.[12]

Kurtis Blow was the first hip-hop artist to have a certified gold single, "The Breaks."

He was also the first rapper to appear on national TV.

Beastie Boys on the Scene

The **Beastie Boys** became the first hip-hop artists to reach large groups of people who weren't African-American. They released their first album, *Pollywog Stew*, in 1982. In 1986 they had their first hit album, *License to Ill*, and the Beastie Boys became the biggest rap act in the world. Hip-hop was now part of the mainstream.

In 2007, Grandmaster Flash and the Furious Five became the first hip-hop artists to be inducted into the Rock and Roll Hall of Fame.

The Beastie Boys helped bring hip-hop to the mainstream.

11 *Not So Simple*

Hip-hop music can be difficult to describe. Today there are more than a dozen different kinds.

Old School

There's old school, which began in the Bronx. It was about good times and party music. DJs liked to play breaks from lots of soul and funk artists. After a while, hip-hop and rap with political themes started to develop. Those songs weren't just for dancing. MCs and DJs chose their words and samples carefully because they wanted to send a message. Sometimes they almost sounded like preachers.

Branching Out

Once hip-hop started to spread beyond the East Coast, new sounds developed. Gangsta rap started on the West Coast in the late 1980s. This rap often sounds angry and includes swearing and talk of violence. It's very different from pop-rap, recorded by *MC Hammer* and groups like *Run-DMC*, which is much lighter and more fun.

MC Hammer's brand of hip-hop was lighthearted and fun.

In the mid-1990s, **OutKast** hit it big with a sound that included a lot of bass, or low notes. It's sometimes called southern rap. At the same time, individual southern cities became known for a special sound. Today Miami is known for party music. Houston is known for a slower sound.

A New Century
The twenty-first century has brought new styles of hip-hop with their own followings. Fans look for specialties like electro-hop, which includes lot of electronic sounds, or Christian hip-hop.

12 *Friendly Rivalries*

There are all kinds of hip-hop competitions. Sometimes individual artists challenge each other. This is all in fun, and it challenges musicians to do their best.

Kanye West and 50 Cent

In the fall of 2007, **50 Cent** and **Kanye West** released new records on the same day. 50 Cent bet that in the first week he would sell more copies of his new record than West could sell of his. (West won, but 50 Cent's sales were big, too.)

In 2007, 50 Cent and Kanye West appear on television to discuss their duel. Which artist would sell more copies of his newly released album?

Scratch-offs

Some scratch artists have organized contests. DJs use their turntabling techniques to develop a five- to six-minute program. They mix and overlay record tracks. Then they get together for a contest. National champions include Filipino DJ **Q-bert**. Another DJ named **DXT** once called Q-bert "a cat with 'bad moves' on the turntable."[13] Q-bert's rival DJs from Southern California were so impressed with his new flavor that they joined up with him. **Mix Master Mike**, **DJ Apollo**, and Q-bert formed the **Invisible Scratch Picklz**.[14]

Dance-offs

There is also a long-standing tradition of hip-hop dance competitions. Break-dance rivalries took hold on the street back in the 1970s. The **Rock Steady Crew**, led by **J. Jo**, and other dance crews challenged each other on the floor. They came up with more moves month after month. These rivalries spurred more energetic and wild styles.

Hip-hop powerhouse Russell Simmons (center) announces his new record label, Russell Simmons Music Group (RSMG).

13 The Record Labels

Both big and small record labels produce hip-hop CDs. A label is a record company. Its goal is to find hot artists and to bring their music to the largest possible audience. Each label has its own style and signs its own kinds of artists.

The Big Ones

Today the biggest hip-hop labels are Bad Boy Entertainment, Death Row, Def Jam, and Interscope. Bad Boy and Def Jam are East Coast studios. Death Row and Interscope are on the West Coast. **Diddy** (Sean Combs) records for Bad Boy. Death Row's biggest stars were **Snoop Dogg** and **Tupac Shakur**. Def Jam has been home to **LL Cool J**, the **Beastie Boys**, and **Public Enemy**. **Eminem** signed with Interscope.

As artists have become rich, some have started their own labels. **Kanye West** has his own label, GOOD Music. **50 Cent** runs G-Unit. **Jay-Z** started his own label, StarRoc, in 2008.

Smaller Scale

Although the major labels produce most of the big hits, there are also many smaller labels putting out hip-hop songs. They're located all over the world. Some are tiny companies that have signed just one or two artists. Some are open for just a year or two and then shut down, often because it takes a lot of money to make and to market a CD. Still, new labels start up all the time.

Diddy (Sean Combs) poses with legendary music producer Quincy Jones (right).

14 *Tale of a Contract*

When hip-hop artists start out, they daydream of the day when they get signed by a label. What few people realize is that signing a contract doesn't mean your career is made.

Tale of an All $tar

Consider this story. For a few years now, there's been buzz about an artist named **All $tar**. All $tar's original name was Jermaine Shute. He grew up in Nashville. He was a troubled teen, but he managed to go to Tennessee State University, where he played basketball. After college, he started to rap. **Yo Gotti**, another rapper, heard him and was really impressed. He helped All $tar score an exclusive contract with an independent label called Cash Money.

In 2005, Cash Money released All $tar's single "Grey Goose," which was such a huge hit that the company had him record an album, *Street Ball*. The engineers mixed and mastered all the music. But three years later, the record hadn't been released. The label wouldn't say why. Hip-hop journalist Kelefa Sanneh, who wrote a story about All $tar for the *New York Times* in February 2008, could only say that hip-hop album sales have been falling lately—just albums, not singles—and label executives don't know how to market them.

All $tar got so frustrated that he decided not to wait for Cash Money to make him a success. He went back to making his own mix tapes, which he promotes and sells himself.[15]

Hip-hop artist All $tar decided to take his career into his own hands.

15 Take One!

What's it like to make a record? Here's how the **Black Eyed Peas**' "Where Is the Love?" came to be. One day the Peas' front man, **will.i.am**, came up with the beat—the drum line. Then he thought of a guitar melody and some words that fit the music. That struck him as a great hook. His friends helped him write the verses.

It Can Take Two

But then will.i.am got stuck. His new song didn't have a chorus. His friend, singer **Justin Timberlake**, came up with one. Timberlake was so excited that he called will.i.am and left a voicemail of a funky recording. He sang his words and beat-boxed in between.

will.i.am and Timberlake worked together to record the song. But it was still missing something. Studio producer Ron Fair went back and added new vocals by **Fergie**. Later, he added a string track. Finally the song was released as the single "Where Is the Love?" It became such a hit that the record company signed the Black Eyed Peas for their first album, *Elephunk*.

Recording takes the work of many people. Even the biggest stars depend on other professionals—musicians, engineers, and producers—to make their hits.

How Sampling Works

Lots of hip-hop music isn't completely original. It includes samples, or short pieces of pre-recorded music. Sometimes hip-hop artists borrow words, instrumental lines, or beats from an earlier song. In 1983, Afrika Bambaataa used the Emulator synthesizer to make the first album that used digital sampling.[16] Today musicians still use electronic samplers when they want to add someone else's sound to their own.

16 Hip-hop in Action

Many hip-hop artists are activists. That means they don't just want to entertain. They also try to influence society and help other people.

Snoop Dogg loves youth football. To give more kids a chance to play and to cheerlead, he founded the Youth Football League for kids in Atlanta. Every year, the season ends with the championship Snooper Bowl.

Music with a Message

Several times, hip-hop artists have come together to make an album to support a cause. One example is *America Is Dying Slowly*, which raised money to help people with AIDS.

Reaching Out

Many hip-hop artists help out the communities where they live or grew up. During the winter holidays of 2007, hip-hop artists helped serve food to the needy in Haverstraw, New York. **Ludacris** created a foundation—an organization that gives money to important causes—called the Ludacris Foundation. It helps kids in Atlanta, Georgia. Record studio executive **Russell Simmons** used part of his fortune to establish the Hip-hop Summit Action Network, which brings young people together. The network's summits have taught young people about financial literacy as well as encouraging them to vote.[17]

There have been other efforts to get out the vote. In 2004, **Diddy** (Sean Combs), **Mary J. Blige**, **50 Cent**, and **Mariah Carey** created a Vote or Die campaign. In February 2008, **will.i.am** wrote "Yes We Can" for Barack Obama's presidential campaign. It became an instant online hit.

⬣17 *Get into It*

Starting right now, there are plenty of ways that you can get into hip-hop.

Turning Your Own Tables

In big cities, you can go to kid-friendly hip-hop concerts. In some cities, summer music camps have special sessions for kids who are interested in hip-hop, who want to get into turntablism, or who want to learn how to use a mixer. Year-round, you should be able to find hip-hop dance lessons. They're offered at dance studios, youth centers, and libraries. There are classes being taught as far away as Tel Aviv, Israel, and Istanbul, Turkey.[18] Also look for writing workshops that focus on rapping or on writing lyrics.

Learning about turntables is a great way to get into hip-hop.

What if you don't live in a big city? Don't feel left out. You can still get involved in the hip-hop scene. Ask around. You'll find out that many adults love hip-hop, too. Teachers use hip-hop music in their classrooms to teach math facts or poetry. At public libraries you can check out hip-hop videos and CDs.

The Next Step

No matter where you live, you can learn about hip-hop on your own. Pick up a pen and try to write a song or rap. If you have a computer, you can buy special software that lets you use samples and loops to produce a demo. As you get better, you might want to perform. Look for talent shows, dance contests, and poetry slams.

Hip-hop dance classes can be found all over the country.

18 For a Living

Wouldn't it be cool to turn your passion for hip-hop into a career? If you're interested, there are many jobs in the field.

On the Stage

Of course you could be a performer—an MC, a DJ, an instrumentalist, or a backup singer. But what if you don't want to be in the spotlight?

Behind the Scenes

Managers take care of entertainers' businesses and sometimes even their personal affairs. **Mathew Knowles**, for example, is a record executive who managed **Destiny's Child** when the group was still together. To this day, he manages the career of his daughter, **Beyoncé**.

Record executive Mathew Knowles works behind the scenes. His daughter, Beyoncé, is more likely to take the stage.

There are also jobs in the recording industry. **Sean Combs** started out as an intern at Uptown Records. He later became the hip-hop performer known as **Diddy**. Now he's a record producer. Other people who work in studios are the mixers and the engineers. Music license specialists work in an office. They try to get permission for musicians to sample other people's music.

A recent high-school graduate prepares for an internship at Def Jam Recordings.

Other hip-hop professionals work on videos. They include producers, dancers, musicians, and video designers.

Share Your Talent

If you're interested in hip-hop style, think about a career in clothing or jewelry design. Artists work on CD covers, posters, and other marketing materials. There are also writers and journalists who specialize in writing about hip-hop.

Glossary

beat-boxed—Used one's mouth to make a sound like a drum or other instrument.

bling—Large, shiny jewelry.

break dancing—A type of dancing that includes energetic steps and acrobatic moves.

breaks—The danceable parts of a song that a DJ plays over and over.

call and response—A musical style in which a singer sings part of a song and then a chorus or audience sings it back.

dashiki—An African shirt or robe.

demo—A sample recording made to show off a performer's new work or talent.

DJs—Short for *disk jockeys*; people who play music on the radio or at a live show.

download—To move a file from the Internet to a computer.

engineers—People who operate the equipment in a music studio.

executives—People who own or manage a company.

layering—The process of adding one sound on top of another.

market—To spread the word about a product in order to encourage people to buy it.

mastered—Made an original recording.

MCs (masters of ceremony)—The people who talk to the audience while the DJ works the turntables.

mixers—Machines used to combine sounds from two turntables; machines used to mix several recorded tracks.

PA system—Public address system, used to broadcast sound in auditoriums or other spaces.

producer—The manager who gets everybody together to record a piece of music.

reggaeton—A style of Latin-inspired music with a fast beat.

remixed—Created new music by combining parts of an older song with new music.

sampling—Taking a part of a song and using it in new music.

slum—A very poor neighborhood.

Time Line

1973 DJ Kool Herc begins to perform at block parties for his friends and neighbors; b-boys start to battle.

1974 DJs start to talk while spinning records; soon there are MCs.

1975 DJ Grand Wizard Theodore invents the scratch.

1977 Graffiti artists paint an entire train—the Christmas train.

1979 Sylvia Robinson founds Sugar Hill Records, which goes on to release "Rapper's Delight," hip-hop's first big hit; Kurtis Blow becomes the first hip-hop artist to get signed by a major record label.

1981 Grandmaster Flash and the Furious Five release "The Message."

1983 The song "Rock It" blends hip-hop and jazz.

1986 Run-DMC has the first rap album ever in the top ten records in the United States; they appear on the cover of *Rolling Stone* magazine.

1989 The Grammys, the American Music Awards, and MTV begin to give out rap awards.

1990 The Fresh Prince (Will Smith) gets his own TV show, *The Fresh Prince of BelAir*.

1991 *Boyz N the Hood*, a popular movie about life in the hip-hop world, is released.

1993 Queen Latifah's third album goes gold; this is the first time this has happened for a female hip-hop artist.

1996 Tupac Shakur is murdered.

2001 Three hip-hop acts start their own clothing lines: OutKast, Snoop Dogg, and Nelly.

2006 The Smithsonian Museum opens a hip-hop exhibit.

2007 The Rock and Roll Hall of Fame acknowledges hip-hop artists for the first time when it inducts Grandmaster Flash and the Furious Five.

End Notes

1. James McBride, "Hip-Hop Planet," *National Geographic*, April 2007, <http://ngm.nationalgeographic.com/ngm/0704/feature4/> (February 13, 2009).

2. *Scratch*, Palm Pictures, 2002.

3. "Hip-Hop Style: What Is Cool?" *PBS*, n.d., <http://www.pbs.org/newshour/infocus/fashion/hiphop.html> (April 15, 2008).

4. Curtis Waller, "Mary J. Blige: It's a Family Affair," *VH1.com*, August 14, 2001, <http://www.vh1.com/artists/interview/1446625/08142001/blige_mary_j.jhtml> (July 20, 2008).

5. Shannon Barbour, "Glow in the Dark Concert," *About.com*, May 4, 2008, <http://rap.about.com/od/concertreviews/fr/GlowInTheDark.htm> (August 8, 2008).

6. "Brooklyn Hip Hop Festival: About," *Brooklyn Bodega*, n.d., <http://www.brooklynbodega.com/brooklynhiphopfestival.htm> (February 13, 2009).

7. "2007 MTV Video Music Awards," *Hip Hop Galaxy*, September 10, 2007, <http://www.hiphopgalaxy.com/2007-Mtv-Video-Music-Awards-hip-hop-5656.html> (April 20, 2008).

8. Jennifer S. Lee, "City Rejects Sale of Building Seen as Hip-Hop's Birthplace," *New York Times*, March 4, 2008, <http://www.nytimes.com/2008/03/04/nyregion/04building.html?scp=15&sq=hip+hop&st=nyt> (April 25, 2008).

9. *Scratch*.

10. Jeff Chang, *Can't Stop Won't Stop* (New York: St. Martin's Press, 2005), pp. 127–129.

11. Ibid, p. 178.

12. *Scratch.*

13. Adisa Banjoko, "The Trigger Man: Face to Face with Mix Master Mike," *Lyrical Words*, n.d., <http://www.lyricalswords.com/articles/mixmastermike.html> (April 25, 2008).

14. Kelefa Sanneh, "Waiting (and Waiting) for a Big Rap Moment," *New York Times*, February 4, 2008, <http://www.nytimes.com/2008/02/04/arts/music/04star.html> (February 13, 2009).

15. Emmett G. Price III, *Hip-hop Culture* (Santa Barbara, Calif.: ABC Clio, 2006), p. 115.

16. Price, pp. 185 and 220.

17. "Hip-hop Dance Classes," *Hip-hop-Dance.net*, n.d. <http://www.hip-hop-dance.net/hip-hop-dance-classes.html> (April 25, 2008).

Further Reading

Books

Hess, Mickey, ed. *Icons of Hip-hop: An Encyclopedia of the Movement, Music, and Culture*. Westport, Conn.: Greenwood Press, 2007.

Kenney, Karen. *Cool Hip-Hop Music: Create and Appreciate What Makes Music Great!* Minneapolis: Abdo, 2008.

Lommel, Cookie. *Russell Simmons*. New York: Chelsea House, 2007.

Web Sites

National Museum of American History—Hip-Hop Won't Stop: The Beat, the Rhythms, the Life
<http://americanhistory.si.edu/news/ factsheet.cfm?key=30&newskey=324>

PBS Independent Lens—Hip-Hop: Beyond Beats & Rhymes
<http://www.pbs.org/independentlens/ hiphop/about_hiphop.htm>

Index